Country
a Shoestring

A picture book for those who yearn for the simpler life

by
Judy Condon

About the Author

Judy Condon is a native New Englander, which is evident in her decorating style and the type of antiques she collects and sells. While Judy's professional career was as an educator, Principal and Superintendent of Schools in Connecticut, her weekends were spent at her antique shop located in Litchfield, Connecticut.

When Judy's husband was relocated to Virginia, she accepted an early retirement from education and concentrated her energy and passion for antiques into a fulltime business. Judy maintains a website, http://www.marshhomesteadantiques.com, and has been a Power Seller on eBay® for over eight years under the name "superct." She has customers throughout the country and has made numerous friends through her extensive internet business.

Judy has five children and five grandchildren. She lives in Spotsylvania, Virginia with her husband and best friend Jeff, with whose support and encouragement, Judy's dreams have materialized.

Judy may be reached through her website or her email address, jbcondon@adelphia.net

Library of Congress Cataloging-in-Publication Data
Country on a Shoestring/by Judy Condon
ISBN-13: 978-0-9772309-0-7
ISBN-10: 0-9772309-0-2

Oceanic Graphic Printing, Inc.
105 Main Street
Hackensack, NJ 07601

Printed in China

Designed and typeset by Lisa Greenleaf
www.greenleafdesignstudio.com

Contents

Chapter One:

This book is for those of us who yearn for the simpler life and want to create that country ambiance on a limited budget. The idea for this book has been in my head for over twenty years. My ideas have been developed through the years of the necessity to decorate on a budget. That is another way of saying that I lacked the money to do all the things I wanted to do or buy! While some have said to me that I am talented and creative, I sincerely believe that I have accomplished things that anyone else is capable of accomplishing! There are a few areas that I admit are out of my realm of ability: I don't do electricity and I don't do heights!

Understandably, the concept "country" is subjective and can mean a variety of things to many people. It can evoke a particular mental image, inspire a love of history, and most certainly stir up an emotional reaction. The concept of "country", to my thinking, is: old, primitive, American, down-home, homemade, homespun, cozy, shabby chic, cottage style, and to some people, junk. I prefer to think of "Country" as a warm and rich feeling inside. It's the smell of apple pie or the feel of a 19thC piece of wood. It's an antique from the 19thC with dry and 'right as right' original 19thC paint.

Those of us who love the feel of country usually spend inordinate amounts of time collecting and gathering. We are always on the hunt; afraid to pass by an antique shop since, after all, the best of the best may be inside. It is something of which we antique addicts never tire. I won't stop for lunch if I'm on the hunt and the shops are open. At 4:45 PM I am still racing to get to that last shop, before it shuts its doors for the night.

The country look can be achieved with flea market finds, 19thC style stencils, old painted furniture, folk art, firkins, game boards, pantry boxes, old-fashioned dolls, quilts, textiles and, of course, displays of endless collections which is anything more than three of a kind! "Country" is inviting, intriguing, and mellow. It is heartfelt. The adage "home is where the heart is" typifies to me the feel that country conveys. "Country" is something from the heart.

Creating that country look does not have to be expensive and I've written *Country on a Shoestring* to prove it. It is very possible to create a country home on a limited budget. I am hopeful that in sharing many pictures and clearly defined "Tips", I can set a spark to your thinking about your own personal country style.

The first half of the book talks about our 1764 home in Litchfield, Connecticut. The house was built by the grandson of the founder of Litchfield, Elijah Marsh. My business, Marsh Homestead Country Antiques, is named after this esteemed man. We had been working with real estate agents for about six months and had given them the parameters of what we were looking for. We wanted an older home, preferably a Cape or Colonial with at least three bedrooms, a quiet street, and a barn if possible. We were exploring an area of the northwest hills of Connecticut one Sunday afternoon and happened down a quiet country dirt road. As we approached the house set on a small knoll overlooking a lovely hillside we knew, without stepping inside, that this was where we would be living.

When my husband Jeff and I purchased our 1764 home in Litchfield, Connecticut, we had little in the way of disposable resources. The house had been recently "renovated" to a style inappropriate for an 18thC home. It was more than livable, but had been modernized in tones of mint green and peach with a great deal of white in the kitchen. I was able to immediately envision what the house needed. Fortunately

I could also recognize that much of what needed to be done could be done with imagination, hard work and courage! The house had a sterile look and lacked the warmth that I was looking for. For two months while we waited to gain occupancy, I created rooms in my mind and had a plan ready to put into action. I definitely had a 'vision' but no means to accomplish it.

I was not raised surrounded by antiques and, in fact, grew up in a home decorated in a modern Danish style. Any "antiques" that had been handed down from my great grandparents or grandparents had long since been given or thrown away. My love for country antiques and an appreciation for the richness of 19thC pine and original paint developed many years after I too had decorated my homes in a formal and traditional manner. It was only through personal change and growth in my life that I truly began to feel in my heart what I wanted to convey in my home.

My first purchase was a cottage pine circa 1860 bureau with rich, warm patina. There is nothing comparable to the feel and smell of old wood! Suddenly, the matched five-piece bedroom suite in dark pine plastic-like veneer with a triple dresser and large headboard held no interest. I was after a totally new "old" look that conveyed the feeling of warmth I felt inside. I began to explore ways to achieve that look on a limited budget.

I took classes in quilting and taught myself how to make 19thC style samplers, which I discovered was a great source of relaxation. I started to hook rugs with only a rug-hooking kit and an instructional tape.

This quilt consisted of 160 Ohio stars and was no easy feat! It wasn't perfect, but that did not detract from the sense of accomplishment I felt when I laid it on the bed.

I have learned a few things over the years! One hint is that any time you are machine stitching your fabric pieces together, don't sew them individually. Instead of cutting the thread, just pull the thread out from the feeder foot and start another fabric piece. You will have approximately twenty pieces on a string. This is a wonderful time saver. Another lesson I learned has to do with size. This particular quilt fits a deep mattress and box spring that, in the past, had always shown beneath the edge of quilts or coverlets. Because we sleep with extra pillows, I was never able to find a bed spread or quilt large enough to cover the double pile of pillows. As a result, I made this quilt so large that it not only covers the pile of pillows, there are about three extra feet in the length! Even in the coldest of winters, the double layer of quilt helps us to stay cozy and warm without a blanket of any kind.

The sampler to the right is one that I adapted from samplers I had seen in magazines. It has a very delicate look to it. I added the border flowers as I went along.

This particular sampler on the left was one of the most challenging I've ever completed. Because it is geometrical, a single error of one stitch would have resulted in the final stitch being off center— something that isn't apparent until that final stitch is sewn.

How appropriate that my first sampler said "Home is where the Heart is"!

This is my first attempt at rug hooking. The loops were too large, and I confused the intended color scheme. The rug is displayed today as a reminder of personal growth.

Here is my second attempt! I enjoyed this particular piece because the colors were luscious.

My husband represents the "practical" side of the family, and while I had dreams of tackling our new home with a vengeance to complete the projects over night, my husband was focusing on those projects with no cosmetic appeal on which most women would rather not spend money. His philosophy of "building the foundation" was evident in the first project we were forced to tackle.

We moved into the house in July 1993 and literally just survived our first winter there. When we called the furnace repairman in the spring, he remarked that it was a blessing that the house had been built in 1764. Without the leaks of fresh air, the carbon monoxide emitted from our ancient furnace would have killed us in an airtight house. Needless to say, I conceded that a 'foundation' project needed to take precedence over my Wish List.

With that crisis behind us, I looked forward to begin working on the kitchen. However, a rough winter had taken its toll on our one-hundred-plus year-old barn and the roof showed signs of stress. It was questionable if the roof would make it through another New England winter. While I didn't agree with the "practical foundation" approach at the time, I now look at the pictures of the old condition of the barn and again have to concede that my husband was right. As in the old barn-raising Amish fashion, we stripped the barn to its rafters and rebuilt the roof in four days. With friends and family, we toiled sunup til sundown, oftentimes by floodlights and occasionally in a passing spring shower.

*Piles of rubble surrounded us.
Even my father-in-law, Jack,
got right into the project. Joe,
who was born in the house
and is now a neighbor, had
to come up for a look.*

*Although I can be seen putting
the final touches on the side,
my primary role for the weekend
was to make sure the crew was
well fed by cooking all the meals.*

*The finishing touch! I supervised
from the ground. If you recall, I
don't do heights!*

With the "foundation projects" behind us, necessity became the mother of invention and courage. The kitchen, which should be warm, welcoming and comfortable, was bland. White vinyl cabinets didn't allow for painting. Periwinkle blue Formica® countertops with matching cabinet knobs made the white cabinets look whiter and the periwinkle blue look bluer! Rippled sheets of yellow

transparent plastic above the counters provided fluorescent lighting while hiding the upstairs plumbing. White linoleum flooring had recently been added and, while fresh and new, required daily washing.

Tip #1 ***Yes, it is possible to paint Formica® countertops.*** My periwinkle blue countertops had a satin finish rather than a high gloss. I lightly sanded them with a small palm sander and painted them with Old Village® Salem Brick Red oil-based paint. For the cost of two quarts of paint, the change was remarkable. I wanted a butcher-block counter but estimates were in excess of $5,000. Instead, I covered the countertops with varied sizes of old cutting boards, which protected

the surface. The effect was actually better than I expected because the aged cutting boards had a richer patina than new wood would have. I created the same butcher-block countertop look and country appeal at a fraction of the cost of a real butcher block countertop.

Tip #2

Reface your cupboards! My cupboard space was exceptional but I did not find the white vinyl exteriors appealing. Each cupboard was equipped with convenient slide-out drawers or shelves, and I didn't want to give up that feature. I removed one of the doors and brought it to a cabinet-maker in town. Again I was trying to achieve a country look while watching my budget. I was looking

for a pine Shaker-style cabinet door. I was quoted $900 for twenty-four paneled doors—unfinished and uninstalled. Instead I finished the doors with two cans of Early American Stain and a gallon of satin finish water-based polyurethane. My husband and I installed all the doors in one evening. Wooden knobs, stained to match, completed the project.

Take up that new floor! I suspected that one of the early, if not original, floor of the house was buried under the linoleum. By looking up at the basement ceiling under the kitchen, I could see the base flooring of the kitchen and dining room. I was able to discern the width of the boards and see that they

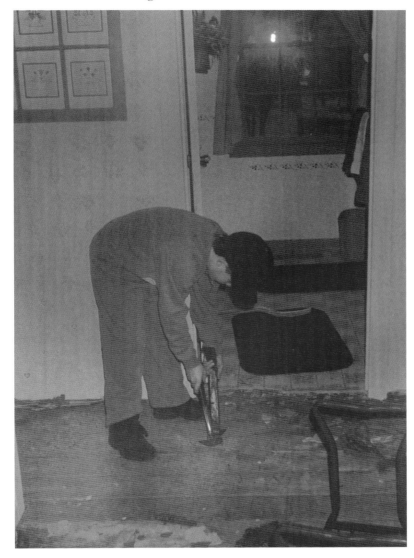

were laid perpendicular to the floors in the rest of the house. Using a crowbar, I removed one corner of the linoleum to only discover several other layers of flooring.

By the time, the family project had been completed, six layers of flooring had been removed to reveal the original pine boards. While this project involved hours of labor, the only expenses were $30 for the belt sander and $19 for a gallon of polyurethane.

Removing the floor became a family project! Even Ryan, my youngest child, quickly learned how to use a hammer and claw!

What a difference the old pine plank floor made. Rather than removing the cupboards to level them for the new floor, we trimmed the cupboard edges and then refaced the cupboards with painted molding to match the countertops. The braided rugs we purchased at an auction for $35 added color, contrast, and warmth.

Tip #4 ***Paint your hardware!*** Rather than replace the door's brass hinges and hardware, I used a can of Rustoleum® flat black paint and spent a few hours painting the brass windows and door hardware. This task was completed with minimal cost, but was a fine detail, that enhanced the country look.

Tip #5

Add window grills! A window without divided light gives a contemporary look and is inappropriate for an 18th or 19thC style home, particularly when there are crank windows involved. I located a source for window grills on the internet, that I painted and installed the grills myself. While grills don't completely replicate a twelve-over-twelve early window, they do add to the aged feeling of the house.

A window with grills is worth the aggravation of painting the grills. You will see my twig holiday tree in the stoneware crock in other pictures. I actually keep it out all year long. It is the first light I turn on each morning when I enter the kitchen.

Tip #6 ***Make your own curtains and save hundreds!*** Even if you aren't a seamstress, it is extremely easy and cost effective to make your own curtains. I selected a variety of plaids and used bolts of unbleached muslin for the lining to minimize fading. I simply measured the length of the window and added 2 inches at either end of the fabric. Placing right sides together, I then sewed the two long and one short side to make a pillow case shape; leaving one end of the short edge

open. Turn the case inside out and press. Taking a final measurement of the window, I measured the fabric from the bottom and pressed the top over to that measurement. A simple hemmed seam on the machine finished the curtains. I tied my curtains back with jute. This further adds to the country look, while again minimizing the projects cost and labor by eliminating the need to make curtain ties.

In the blue guest room below I simply tied a loop with jute in the corner of the windows and let the fabric hang. This allowed a larger window space for guests to view the lake.

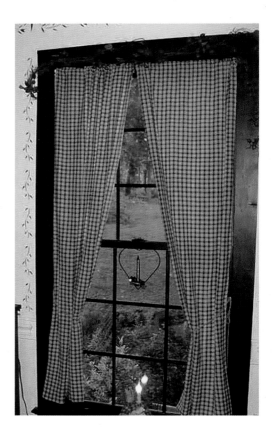

For the small window over the kitchen counter, an old flour seed sack is secured with a tack and jute in the corner and center. A wooden pole suspended with "S" hooks hangs over the window and displays an old corn husk holder with faux apples, a miniature buttocks basket, and a cluster of dried gourds.

Tip #7 ***Conceal upstairs plumbing!*** In a 19thC house, it can be difficult to conceal 20th century "new" plumbing. I replaced the rippled plastic light covering above the counter with pine boards that were cut to length. I then stained and

nailed them perpendicularly across the frame. My husband, (Remember, I don't do electricity or heights!) drilled a hole in one of the boards and wired the black wrought-iron light fixture I had purchased at a flea market.

This picture shows it all: the new lighting arrangement, the Old Salem Brick paint, window grills, curtains with jute ties, and the cutting-board counters!

Tip #8

Use brick to add age! The picture on the preceding page showing my daughter Julie shows the counter with a white painted wooden base. In order to blend the cupboard exterior bases with the Salem Brick Red painted counters and trim, I bought from a local quarry, half bricks made by EZ Brick®. I applied a concrete gray adhesive with the consistency of a gritty frosting to the bricks. As a matter of fact, using a putty knife to apply the adhesive was very much like frosting a cake. I started at the bottom because the weight of the bricks with the adhesive will cause the bricks to slide. Just one word of caution; I recommend applying one or two horizontal rows at a time and allow sufficient time for the rows to set and dry before setting the next row. I had set a number of rows from the bottom before allowing each row to set. The weight of the bricks and the smooth horizontal surface, caused the bricks to all cluster on the bottom of the wall. As a result, I was forced to use duct tape to hold the individual bricks in place to keep them from sliding to the bottom of the wall while the adhesive dried.

The picture on the right shows the wall over the counter The picture below shows the newly applied brick base and painted countertop.

Prior to my retirement as a Superintendent of Schools, there would be an occasional day when my office closed due to inclement weather. On one such day, my husband had left on a business trip and had said goodbye to me in the dining room, where there sat our lovely 19thC Stepback cupboard.

The ceiling in the dining room is post-and-beam construction and is original to the house. The previous owners had placed acoustical ceiling tile between the rafters. I began removing the tiles before the owners reached the end of the driveway!

The door to the left leads to a small narrow porch, which was added to the house in 1917. Our neighbor, Joe, remembered when the room had been built, but couldn't recall what it had been used for. For that reason, we always referred to it as the "whatever" room.

I regretted that one of the previous owners had either sealed up or totally removed three fireplaces, one of which was a beehive that, over the years, evolved into a walk-in pantry. Unfortunately, the addition of the "whatever" room made restoring a working fireplace in the dining room impossible.

Add a fireplace! It is possible to create the illusion of a fireplace for decorative purposes very easily and in little time! My unsuspecting husband was not gone one hour when I began to remove the chair railing and baseboard on the wall where I intended to "build" my fireplace. In the basement I had an old mantel that I found at a flea market for $50. I measured its width against the wall and centered it, marking the wall on either side. Using 3 inch long nails from a previous building project, I nailed the mantel directly to the wall. I reattached the chair rail and baseboard molding after I cut them to fit in the smaller space on either side of the mantel.

The mantel immediately provided an opportunity for decorating and added a charm to the room itself; however, it still lacked the authentic appearance that a used fireplace would have. Using leftover half bricks from the kitchen project, I applied those to the interior space of the mantel authenticating an old fireplace that had been sealed. To give the bricks a further aged and sooted look, I used flat

black spray paint and quickly swirled black spray across the face of the bricks. By the time my husband arrived home from his trip that evening, I was finished with my fireplace project. While he approved and liked the results, his only comment was, "I see you had a little spare time on your hands today!"

The real irony occurred two years later when we were relocated to Virginia and had to sell our home. I was indirectly complimented when the Home Inspector from the bank inspected our home for a pending mortgage. The Home Inspector wrote in his report: "There are two fireplaces in the home. One is operational; however, the second fireplace could not be determined to be in working order as it has been sealed off!"

Tip #10 ***Paint your roof in a day!*** Keeping in mind that this is a book that provides tips for decorating or redecorating "on a shoestring", the roof of our home presented a unique challenge to me. The Desert Sand tan color of the roof shingles had discolored over fifteen years and while the sun had bleached it in the front, the shade had stained it in the back.

In addition, tan was not a roof color I would have selected for our white house. The contrast between the roof and house was pale and the tan did not complement our barn that was painted New England Red. I gathered reroofing estimates justifying the project as being a "foundation project," because the roof was approaching the end of its lifespan. The quotes came back in excess of $5000, making the project impossible to undertake. I had recently completed a roof replacement at one of my schools. So I contacted the General Manager of the construction company to inquire if, by any chance, it was possible to paint a shingled asphalt roof. I could tell by the pause on the other end of the phone that the contractor was aghast at my question.

The next day I received a call from the General Manager saying that when he passed along my question to another contractor, he was informed that, in fact, there was a roof paint. He provided me with a few company names that could be found on the internet. I learned that the paint came in only five colors and could only be ordered in quantities of five-gallon drums. The colors were red, green, white, dark brown, and black. Since I wanted a charcoal gray roof, my limited color selections presented a further challenge. We ordered a five-gallon drum of white and one of black. Over the course of three weeks, my husband sampled various proportions of each color in miniscule quantities until we were able to mix the charcoal gray color we wanted. We now had the "formula" for the ratio of black to white paint and now just needed to find someone we could hire to apply it. If you recall from the start, I don't do electricity and I don't do heights.

One Saturday, my son Dick, and a friend, mixed the formula in a large trash container and applied the paint with a roller. It took only one day to apply the first coat. On Sunday, a second coat was applied. We stopped traffic on our quiet country road that day and people marveled as the house took on a completely different appearance before their very eyes. For a little over $300, not only had we changed the color of our roof and improved the house's esthetic appearance but, we also had extended the roof's lifetime by applying a protective coating to the asphalt shingles.

Tip #11

Replace vanity tops with "aged" wood! Our main floor bathroom was outdated and unfortunately quite visible since it was directly off the kitchen. The bathroom consisted of a Formica® covered vanity, an old mirrored metal medicine cabinet, a blue sink, and a long bar of large round light bulbs for lighting. We replaced the vanity with an unfinished vanity that I stained with Early American stain. Again, using satin finish polyurethane, I applied one coat to protect the

wood. Like other bathrooms that I have renovated, I substituted a top with a piece of unfinished laminated pine purchased at Lowe's for approximately $10. Using the template packaged with the sink, I cut the hole in the top, and affixed the vanity top to the sink with epoxy. The change was remarkable.

I used this same process to replace vanity tops in other bathrooms. In place of a backboard, I stenciled the ceiling border pattern across the back of the sink.

Tip #12 *Use that ogee mirror in a whole new way!* I have lived in a number of houses that have had a recessed medicine cabinet over the bathroom sink. Never, did the medicine cabinet match the pine vanity top. I discovered that a recessed medicine cabinet is quite easy to remove once its door is off. A recess is left into which you can build your own shelves. I chose to build the shelves so that the finished piece looked like a bookcase, I then inserted the entire piece into the

recess. I took an early ogee pine mirror and attached hinges to one edge. Next, I then attached the hinges to the recessed side of my shelves. Only those of us in the family knew that the lovely 19thC pine ogee mirror concealed a medicine cabinet.

An Ohio tinsmith crafted the tin wall sconces and hanging light reflected in the mirror.

Tip #13 *Increase your display space!* Typical of an 18thC home, the rooms were small. This minimized the space for furniture and space to display my numerous collections. Remember, a collection is anything more than three of a kind! Using simple 1" X 3" X 12' pineboards, I screwed one pine board to the top edge of the other to create an "L" shaped shelf. I used numerous screws, (most likely MANY more than necessary,) I painted the shelves prior to nailing them into the walls. I placed the shelves around the perimeter of my living room which instantly added approximately fifty feet of display area, without compromising comfort or floor space. By lowering the visual height of the ceiling, the shelves also added warmth and coziness to the room.

Dark hunter green paint is used on all the moldings, accented with deep New England reds. Baskets, lanterns, and dried flowers adorn the original 1764 chestnut beams and posts.

The clock to the right was given to us by my husband's mother. It is a Boardman Wells all wooden gear clock dating back to the mid-19thC. It requires winding twice daily and holds a special place in our list of priceless treasures. The maker painted the glass front as an exact representation of the gold pendulum.

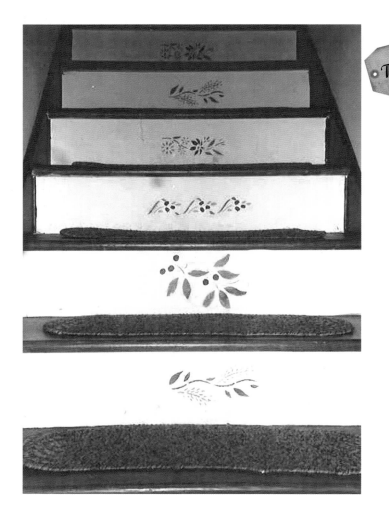

Tip #14

Age your stairs! Wall-to-wall carpeting, particularly in a mint green color, on the stairs leading to the second floor from the living room did not fit into my plans. At no cost, I removed the carpet, used a palm sander to "clean" up the stair treads, and painted the back of the stairs with a flat off-white paint. I then stenciled the back of each tread in a different pattern; pulling together the overall affect by repeating the use of the colors.

I later added braided treads for color!

Tip #15 ***Replace sliding doors with French doors!*** The backside of our home had an extension, which was actually an old carriage shed. The shed was used for storing firewood back in the late 19thC. It was also used for slaughtering pigs, according to our neighbor Joe. A previous owner had installed sliding glass doors along the wall where the door to the carriage shed had been.

The original carriage shed can be seen in this picture taken in the early 1940's. All of the outbuildings and pond were gone by the time we purchased the home. In the early 1900's the house was a dairy farm. The stonewall along side the driveway can be seen in the more recent pictures and still stands today. The "whatever" room is seen on the side above the entrance to the cellar door that retained its late 18thC hardware. At the end of the shed, a doorway leads to the milk house where milk was stored before adequate refrigeration was available. It still stands today and is still the coolest place on the block in the heat of summer.

The door to the milk house can be seen at the back of the room.

While the sliders allowed a great amount of light, they minimized the much-needed wall space. I purchased at a flea market two old sides of a French door that required extensive work. I removed layers of paint from the panes that were still present and re-glazed the glass. My local hardware/lumber store hung the doors and created the frame. This project saved over $1500 compared to a new double hung set of French doors.

Everything looked better with the French doors! We still kept a great deal of light in the room.

You can see on the doorknobs, plates and hinges where flat black paint has enhanced the look.

Chapter Two:

In 2002, my husband was relocated to Virginia, leaving me with mixed emotions. Moving closer to our grandchildren was the primary attraction to the major change in our life; however, the move also meant I had to resign my position as Superintendent of Schools with a district in which I had invested an inordinate amount of emotional energy and leave many fellow employees and associates with whom I had enjoyed working. As I had never lived outside of Connecticut, it meant leaving many lifelong friends and moving away from my elderly parents.

Our five children are grown; three married, one single, and one in college. Despite the fact that they had all left the nest, they were surprised that we would ever leave the home on which we had worked so hard and which was truly Home.

My husband's new position in Virginia dictated somewhat the parameters of where we would live as well as our intent to be near enough to the grandchildren so that making visits and sharing celebratory events where plausible.

After months of searching for an older home, we abandoned the idea because of the cost and geographic parameters made it impossible to find what we were looking for. We then agreed that if an older farmhouse was not in our future, we would like to live near the water. We were fortunate to find a large newer colonial home in excellent condition and with a great deal of "country potential".

We purchased our home in April of 2002, but were unable to move into it because I had agreed to complete my contractual obligations in Connecticut. This delay also gave us two months to complete some projects that were best done while the house was empty.

We hired our thirty-five year old son for a three-week period to complete three major projects. Our immediate goal was to remove all door, window, and baseboard moldings and paint all the walls an off-white rather than the bright white that was used from top to bottom throughout the house. Both of these projects paved the way for the change that resulted in the greatest overall difference.

Tip #16

Age those floors! The pictures below show the living room, when we purchased the home. While the floors were lovely, (and quite expensive I later learned!), they did not have the feel or warmth to complement my 19thC antiques.

Create the country charm of "aged" pine wide floorboards at one-tenth the cost of most flooring materials. Laying down a random length pine floor is a relatively easy and fast process when you follow a few tips. I prefer using raw pine, one inch by ten inch wide; however, six-or twelve inch wide may also be used depending on the size of the room. A three-inch wide board looks better in a smaller room, such as a bathroom. I have both replaced and applied directly over existing flooring, a wood floor with rich patina and one that looked as though it had withstood the tests of time.

The first step is to remove all moldings; baseboards, doors, and door trim. Random lengths of pine were cut, fitted and nailed directly over the existing floor. Having installed a number of wooden floors with my son, we had learned a few tricks over the years. For instance don't nail any boards until the entire row

is laid and fitted. This allows for flexibility and change if an adjustment is necessary. Start at the edge of the room that is farthest away from the entrance. There is more room for adjustment on that last board where the entrance to the room meets another floor. I use flathead nails purchased by the pound as opposed to reproduction rose head nails. While rose head nails will authenticate the floor more than new flat head nails do, I have learned through experience that their raised surface makes cleaning difficult, as mops will catch on the nail head. Rose head nails are also not very comfortable to walk on with bare feet. If children are in the house, I strongly recommend that rose head nails not be used.

A rag can be used to apply the stain but I have found that a sponge mop works just as well and is a great deal easier on your back. I have always used Early American stain by Miniwax.

A large floor can be stained with the mop in a matter of an hour. Let it dry for an hour and then apply a single coat of water-based polyurethane. Use the water-base matte finish to keep shine to a minimum. By the next morning, rugs can be placed and furniture moved into place.

The finished pine floor with one coat of Early American Stain and one coat of satin finish, water base, polyurethane.

Some might object to the hammer marks. But to my thinking, I believe they add to the aged look of the floor.

The finished floor with a vintage wool braided rug from my husband's grandmother.

The bedrooms required little preparation. However, the upstairs hall presented a problem in that the rooms feeding into the hallway now had wide pine floorboards. They were also at the same level as the existing floor, which was a type of high-gloss narrow board engineered wood. I also wanted the floor in the landing to abut the base of the stair railing.

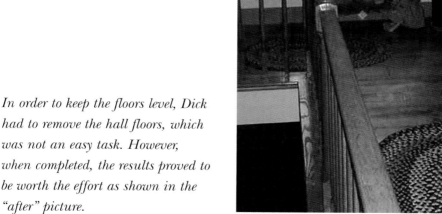

In order to keep the floors level, Dick had to remove the hall floors, which was not an easy task. However, when completed, the results proved to be worth the effort as shown in the "after" picture.

The floors added a rich look to the upstairs hall landing. The landing now blended with the large dollhouse built in 1923 by my great-grandfather for my mother when she was a child.

The porcelain china on the table to the right is Limoge from France.

The miniature loom was made especially for my mother and is an actual working loom!

o Tip # 17 ***Don't be put off by concrete floors!*** A wide plank pine floor can be installed over any surface, including concrete! It simply takes one relatively easy extra step. Since it is not possible to nail pine boards directly onto a concrete surface, the first step is to create a grid similar to the one shown below with furring strips. These strips are sold in bundles and are very inexpensive. Place the strips six inches apart and use an air-pressure gun to nail the furring strips to the concrete. The furring strips should be placed perpendicular to the direction you want your finished boards to lie.

Folded newspaper can be used between the strips to minimize any potential squeaks.

Your floor will begin to look like this as it falls into place.

We saved the floor in the front hall entrance until the end. I was concerned that this would be one of those projects where I might have to call in a professional to "clean up my mess". The front hall flooring was white ceramic tiles which provided a bright entrance and enhanced the light from the large bay window at the end of the hall.

Although the ceramic tiles provided light, the tiles inhibited the visual continuity of the wide board floors on the main level.

I was concerned that even if we could remove the tiles, the sub-flooring might not be the same level as the rest of the flooring. With hammer in hand, we took the leap of faith and began our project. Within two hours, we had shattered and removed all the tiles. The new plank floor blended perfectly with the rest of the abutting rooms.

This is the view upon entering the front door of the house. The lake is straight ahead.

Creative ways for display! There are numerous ways to expand your display space without compromising comfort. I discovered that one or two old shutters, hinged to a window on the interior molding provides space to hang country pieces and to mix textures. The shutter below is one I change with the seasons. The chair is visible at eye level. The doll and wreath soften the hard surface of the shutter.

My friend Kathy Lombardi, whose many items I sell in my shop and use to decorate my home, crafted the Raggedy Ann dolls. Kathy was commissioned by the White House to create ornaments for the holiday tree. Her work is extraordinary in expertise, style, imagination, and the fine details she adds to each item. You'll see samples of Kathy's workmanship throughout this book.

The color of the shutter really isn't important. Here the dark green blends with the Pearwood paint and navy check curtains. I look for dry paint. My preference is a painted surface that is aged and has no shine.

This view of the master bedroom from the hall entrance shows the finished floor, cottage pine bureau and one of the many 19thC pine ogee mirrors scattered around the house.

This cupboard was found in Vermont. It holds a miniature feather tree which holds suspended family photos. My mother's baby shoes sit on the first shelf.

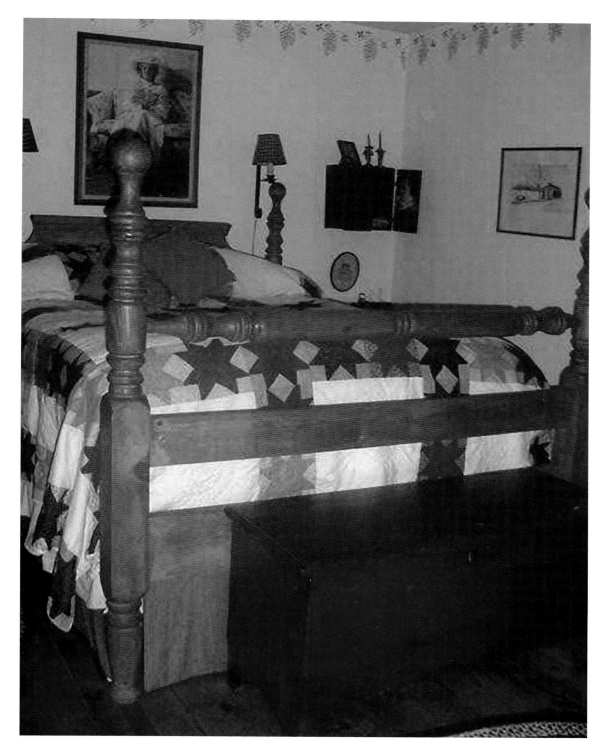

The four-poster pine cannonball queen-size bed was purchased from a retail store. We stripped down and refinished the bed to give it an older look. The chest at the foot of the bed is a 19thC cherry piece we found in Massachusetts. The oil portrait over the bed is a painting of me in my wedding dress.

I also enjoy using shutters as backdrops on walls. Because shutters have usually been weathered over time, their dry surfaces and colors are often unique. The blue of this shutter is rich and is enhanced by the colors of gold in the dried flower wreath.

This shutter, found in a barn in Maine, was $10. It's adorning the guest room that we call the "blue room" I've decorated this room in blues and have accented it with mustard accessories.

Here is the blue room in summer with a lightweight woven linen spread.

Above pictured is the blue room in winter. Braided rugs in blues surround the spool bed which was found in upstate New York for $75! The ecru quilt on the bed is a reproduction. The three ticking textile covered pillows were purchased at an antique show in northern Virginia. The bench at the foot of the bed in dry original robin's egg blue is a perfect spot to display a graduated stack of reproduction fabric covered pantry boxes that were crafted by Kathy Lombardi. The blue measure from Maine is filled with vintage authentic large rag balls in varying shades of blue. These ragballs were found in Pennsylvania.

A small piece of peg board in 19thC robin's egg blue paint displays a replica homespun apron and bonnet.

An old tool chest found in New Hampshire in robin's egg paint is nailed to the wall in the blue room. It's a unique piece with a superb surface. Hanging it on the wall gives me another display space and the fact that it creates three shelves is a bonus!

An old bucket bench in original mustard paint was found in Pennsylvania. It never made it into the shop for resale! The bench fits perfectly under the hall's cathedral window, without blocking light. It provides a resting spot for a bear and a primitive folk art doll.

I couldn't resist using the early child's wagon in dry red wash as another way to display dolls! The wagon fits perfecting in the living room with its barn reds and Windsor greens. Hidden behind the chair, the display is out of the line of traffic but is still visible upon entering the room.

An early 20thC doll carriage is a perfect spot for one of Kathy's dolls to rest.

This is the living room as you enter it from the back of the house. The 19thC blanket chest in original red wash was found in a barn in Maine.

The deep mantel provides space for one of my collections. My German stick-legged sheep blend right in with the Noah's Ark. The lantern on the left is an authentic early piece that still retains its original reflector mirror. The 19thC dated oil portrait, found in New Hampshire, is actually one, of a set of twin brother portraits.

A 19thC Stepback cupboard from Maine
in original red paint houses a number of
German Noah's Arks from my collection.

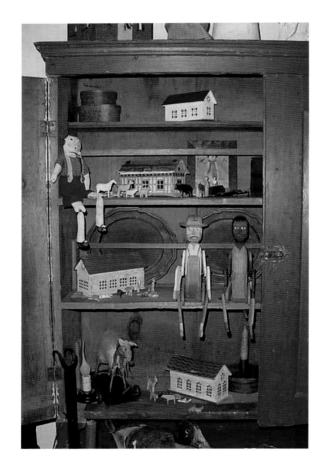

A Pinocchio articulated doll
sits on the Stepback shelves.

The tin goose was found in Maine.

The living room as seen from the front hall entrance looking toward the lakeside of the house. Behind the chairs sits Milo Washington who is also pictured on the right in an early mustard paint child's chair.

Silhouetted against the bay window, a 19thC rocking horse from Maine sits atop an early square nailed pine blanket chest.

A miniature electrified General Store sits atop the double door 19thC pine cupboard.

The lighted candle shop to the left and the lighted New England Cape Cod house below were crafted by Maine artist, Guy Paulin.

A small child's bench in early green paint provides a place at the top of the stairs for three dolls to greet overnight guests.

An old milk bottle carrier found at a Farmer's Market in Pennsylvania is mounted on the kitchen wall. It's ideal for displaying miniatures. Each piece has a story!

*An original mustard painted peg rack
hangs on the wall of the hall entrance.
Three Shaker homespun bonnets and
a seedbag are displayed. The seedbag
is filled with white beans for effect.*

*Even an 18thC door makes a lovely
background for display. This 18thC
door leads to nowhere! The paint and
hardware are original. I nailed the door
to the wall so that it appears to be a
closet and use the surface to decorate
seasonally.*

The bowl rack in the dining room was easy to make on a small jigsaw and cost $15 for materials. Dough bowls in paint are colorful against the 19thC blue cupboard found in Virginia. The bowl of faux pears further adds color and contrast. The porcelain pitcher was hand painted by my great aunt.

Berry garlands everywhere! I have found that garlands are one of the most inexpensive ways to add charm and warmth to almost every room. A berry garland of red and burgundy is used in almost every room. A six-foot strand can be purchased for $10-$12. Some ways to use the strands are shown on the following page. Although not shared in this book, white berry garlands, that are draped on the holiday tree give the tree a lovely appearance of snow-filled branches.

A strand of faux-red rosehips garland on a twig-like branch pictured below is used in the living room to brighten the hunter green molding of the window. Notice how the garland picks up the red in the stencils.

Faux Williamsburg fruit garlands were put up in the dining room for my November Holiday Sale/Open House and were never taken down!

The tray ceiling was the final area in the kitchen to finish. Burgundy berry garlands mixed with blueberry vines were the answer. They added texture and color without compromising the space.

The hanging iron fixture was brought from Connecticut.

This is the dining room as we first saw it. The picture below shows the room as it begins its transformation. Painted moldings and grills in Old Village Antique Pewter paint are the final dressings of the room!

Tip #20 *You can't go wrong with stencils!*

Stencils are an inexpensive tool to use to bring a room together. They visually pull colors together while accenting others – and stenciling is easy to do. The most important hint is to use a dry brush! When we started to repaint the dining room, it was white from top to bottom. We "warmed up" the room considerably with the use of Old Village® Antique Pewter paint on the trim. Antique Pewter is a color that changes depending on what objects are close and by the time of day. Sometimes it looks gray and sometimes it looks sage green. I use this color with deep country red and then pull the colors together with stencils. In the dining room, I've also added mustard to the stencil. This allows me to introduce accessories with a mustard color.

The finished room with color! Note the remarkable difference the stencils make here and in the two pictures that follow.

An old door in original blue paint
that is nailed to the wall, gives the
illusion of a recessed cabinet.

The living room, minus the
stencil is nearly finished.

Note the remarkable warmth that was created after the stencil was added.

The pine jelly cupboard on the left was a wedding present from my husband's family. The double measure on top in old blue is always filled with flowers. The unique yellowware jug with blue band on the table is filled with lilacs. The table, found in Maine, is square nailed and retains almost all of its original red paint.

Tip #21

Buyer beware! In my shop and on eBay®, I try very hard to offer an assortment of country pieces to accommodate a wide range of country tastes and country pocketbooks. I have located sources for high-end reproduction pieces which, when integrated with authentic pieces, complement each other at a fraction of the cost. For example, the candlestick, pictured on the following page, on the corner of the Stepback cupboard is sold in my shop for $40. I saw the exact same piece marked "$1050 firm" in a high-end antique shop. Many reproductions are so authentic-looking that the adage "buyer beware" has taken on a whole new relevance!

I have mixed reproduction pewter with authentic old pewter, demonstrating that many people would be hard pressed to tell the difference between the pieces.

The mirrored wall sconce is another popular country accessory and is an excellent representation of an 18thC piece. This delightful sconce sells for $45 and looks lovely next to the authentic 19thC large cupboard in original red wash. When I purchased the cupboard, it was covered with thick white porch paint. A heat gun was used to bubble and remove the paint. What a delight to find the exceptional 19thC red wash beneath.

A customer in my shop once asked why this sampler below on the left was priced at $65 while the one on the right was $650? It is near impossible to tell without close scrutiny that the one on the left is a paper print and the one on the right is an authentic signed 1786 silk thread on linen.

In our second guest room, the "green room" wall enables me to display many of my samplers They are mixed with old and new as well as originals I created.

The spool headboards were found at a flea market. They are "sitting" free-style on the side rails of the frame. The matching twin quilts were made by a friend of my mother's grandmother and are hand pieced and heavily hand quilted.

I've mixed old and new signs! The Supper Here Today 5-7 sign was found in Maine many years ago and is my favorite. The day we moved to Virginia, the movers showed up on our front door step with this sign in their hands!

Someone once asked me to name my favorite collection. I couldn't answer it! I have no favorite but enjoy each and every one. Some collections have higher monetary values than others, but my enjoyment of each comes without a price tag. Just as I have mixed sampler prints with authentic linen samplers, I have

also mixed silhouettes with silhouette replicas. I utilize the replicas as "fill-ins" until I can replace them with an original. Oftentimes, I keep the replica as it is as pleasant as an original.

The silhouette on the bottom is one of my daughter when she was ten. The determining factor in this grouping is the black frames, which tie the variety of objects together.

We left the stairs as they were when we moved in. They're easy to clean and they maintain their wood tone. Below, handmade braided stair treads in tones of gold and green perfectly match the wheat stenciling in the hallway.

This is a sampling of my gameboard collection. I change the boards as new ones are found. The game boards enhance an otherwise drab stairway that is instantly viewed from the front door.

This is the view from the upstairs landing looking down.

Although not wooden, this early gameboard has a marvelous tin surface with superb original paint.

Tip #22 ***Paint the cupboards!*** In the Fall 2003, *Small Rooms Decorating* magazine featured my kitchen in their publication. I wrote an article entitled "Aged to Perfection." The pictures below are what my kitchen looked like when we purchased the house. By the end of our closing day the aging process had begun. Having practiced once in Connecticut, I knew exactly what had to be done to make my kitchen look like a 19thC room. The kitchen cupboards were painted Salem Brick Red by Old Village®.

By the end of the first day in our home, the kitchen was already beginning to look more 19thC because of red cupboards. Applying pine floorboards necessitated the moving of the stove. It was a relatively easy process as the boards were laid down directly over the existing flooring.

With the cupboards painted and the floors in place, I tackled the chore of cementing half bricks to the back splash, counter ends and around the windows. This is a project that can be accomplished within hours and with relatively little cost. The results are monumental as you can see from the pictures below.

I started applying the half bricks at the counter ends, as I had done in my kitchen in Connecticut. Heeding my own advice, I set only a few rows at a time. With the ends done, I cemented half bricks to the back splash and around the windows. The cost of the project was approximately $200 for the brickwork.

The tray ceiling was left bare for months since I couldn't decide how I wanted to treat it. I had wanted to stencil it but was concerned that the room would be overcome with stencils. Instead burgundy berry garlands mixed with blueberry vines were the answer.

The 19thC washtub in old dry red wash and square nails made the perfect island for display and added country charm at the same time. Early painted firkins sit under the washtub, tucked out of the way. The large yellowware bowl belonged to my grandmother. It is typically filled with varieties of bright faux fruit appropriate for the season.

Tip #23

You can't fit another thing in here! Every time my mother visits, she remarks, "You can't fit another thing in this house!" When space is at a premium, I've created ways to increase display area in my kitchen by adding dimension or by utilizing small spaces.

The 19thC cricket bench in original soldier blue paint provides an additional shelf for a small lamp, berry candle, and yellowware hen.

The Shaker 19thC sifter in original black paint sits next to a small working butter churn in original red wash.

The mixer belonged to my grandmother and dates to the 1940's. I still use it today for all my baking.

The square pole suspended from the ceiling by "S" hooks holds a display of dried flowers, a small buttocks basket, and a miniature sieve in blue paint.

The Shaker bucket in robin's egg blue holds a collection of rolling pins. It also holds a treasured pillow made by a friend which says, "Friendship is a Sheltering Tree".

I added a small faux fireplace in the dining room so I could display another Noah's Ark and some of my many German stick-leg sheep. The painting on an old cutting board above was created by Guy Paulin in Maine.

The windowsill in the "tree house" room gave me more display space for Kathy's animals.

Tip #24 *Think pink?* Or not! It is possible to age a pink marbled bathroom for less than $2,000. While a "picture will speak a thousand words," the transformation of the master bath deserves some explanation. You can see from the initial picture that the overall predominant color was pink: a pink tub, a pink shower, pink

matching sinks, pink wall-to-wall carpet, and pink variegated marble vanity tops. The jacuzzi was incased in pink variegated linoleum. What a view though!

As much as I am willing to plunge in and tackle challenges, painting the tub and shower was not part of my repertoire. I located a professional who, for $1400, enameled both the shower and Jacuzzi in a light almond paint. In twenty-four hours, we were able to use them both! Please note, only one product can be used to clean an enameled bathroom. Check with your local paint supplier.

Occasionally I come up with an idea that turns out to be the most cost effective of any and gives me the greatest pleasure when it is completed. I wanted to achieve a granite look to the jacuzzi, and for $37, I did it!! I purchased self-sticking vinyl textured floor squares from a major national home center. I used an epoxy on the back to reinforce the adhesive to a "polished" surface. I used scissors to cut the squares around the fixtures. First I made a template with a piece of paper and then I traced the template onto the tile for cutting. Along the edge, I used paint to tie in with the gray "grout" of each square.

I replaced the old glass in the shower and used opaque glass on the front and right side, I used clear glass on the left side so that a panoramic view of the lake while showering is possible.

I achieved the results I was looking for by adding my collection of birdhouses and a few plants. My total cost? $37! The gray tin goose on the windowsill ties in with the gray tones of the faux granite on the surround.

With the completion of the tub and shower projects, I was ready to tackle the vanity. I removed the brass knobs on the vanity. I then used Old Village® Pear Wood paint to paint the vanity and moldings around the baseboards and doors.

I purchased a piece of unfinished laminated pine at a local lumber yard and cut two holes using the template that came with the sinks.

Prior to installing the sinks, I removed the mirror. I then stained the pine top with Early American® stain and applied a coat of polyurethane for protection. After the top was dry, I dropped in the sinks and added new fixtures.

We've come to appreciate the "modern" conveniences we didn't have in our authentic 1764 house! It's a treat to have double sinks in the bathroom and lots of electrical outlets throughout the house.

The pine ogee mirror, found in Massachusetts, fit perfectly over the double vanity. Adding cobalt blue stencils and sconces on either side of the mirror really warmed up the room.

The reproduction sconces flanking
the large 19thC pine ogee mirror
are a popular item at Marsh Homestead
Country Antiques. Reproduction
18th or 19thC lighting is popular
because of the cost of authentic
early lighting.

Tip #25

Turn it around! There are many ways to utilize country accessories. While the serious collector wouldn't consider purchasing a piece that was not in mint condition, the average collector might and then upgrade in the future. I have found wonderful "flawed" items and have used them in my home at a fraction of the cost. This has occasionally earned me the nickname "The Queen of Placement"!

I purchased this beautiful 19thC cobalt glazed ovoid crock for $30 at an antique shop in Connecticut. In mint condition, this piece would sell for approximately $600 or more. I was able to purchase it for $30 because there was a huge crack in the back! My tip: turn it around! The fact that it is cracked does not detract from the pleasure I derive every time I see it. I can even use it for holding cut flowers by simply placing a glass or plastic container inside the crock to hold water.

These firkins are not all perfect and the prices I paid would support that! Turn it around! If there is a broken handle or stave, no one has to know but you. Also, it is very difficult and time consuming to find the exact size for a graduated stack. So, until you do find it, push the firkin a little off-center and you will create an illusion of a graduated stack.

Tip #26 *Buy that Firkin without the lid!*

Don't pass that firkin by just because it is missing its lid! Lidless firkins make great wastebaskets, containers for rolled-up towels or plant containers. And they are a fraction of the cost!

This chippy white painted firkin right was only $40! If it had had a lid, it would have cost over $350! In the holiday season, I fill it with a poinsettia.

This stack of firkins is one that I keep for myself and change occasionally as I upgrade or find needed sizes.

No one would know that the large deep Windsor green firkin on top of the cupboard doesn't have a lid.

A firkin without a lid makes a nice holder for rolled towels in the bathroom or for use as a wastebasket.

Tip #27 ***Never walk away from a good cutting or dough board!*** Good dough boards are priceless! I stockpile them and sometimes trade off some on my counters for others I've purchased. You have seen that they cover my countertops! I love the look of the patina AND I have no fear of burning the countertop or damaging it with a sharp knife.

For $300 at a flea market I purchased the 19thC standing butter churn in original red wash pictured on the left. It has the crank but no top. With a dough board large enough to fit the top, I've got a great, spacious end table in the living room for pennies!

Note the carrier with apples on the table. For $15, I added color and something unique.

The other table worth mentioning in the living room is an old sewing base that someone was throwing away. I added a dough board on the top and created a spacious end table.

The bureau on the right certainly looks like it has authentic 19thC red wash, but it doesn't! I used red powdered milk paint mixed with water from D.O. Siever Products® in Pennsylvania. I applied the paint with a brush. After it dried, I rubbed Brie® wax over the entire piece and rubbed off a considerable amount on the top to expose the bare wood. This bureau sits in the green guest room and matches the spool headboards that were also painted with red powdered milk paint!

My point is that any piece of furniture can be made to look old if you know how to do it. If you are a "purist", this method would not be appealing. But it allows the average collector to decorate "on a shoestring" and have a nice piece of furniture until the authentic piece can be found and afforded.

Tip #28

Keep lots of paintbrushes on hand! I buy paintbrushes by the box for $12. They are great for quick projects. I keep two for touch-ups on the water-based wall paint and I just rinse the brushes after each use.

This summer porch was converted into a finished room for the price of $150 for pine boards for the floor and a gallon of paint. When we moved in, this room had aluminum slide windows with plywood unpainted walls and deck flooring. It was not insulated and was located off the kitchen overlooking the lake.

Our initial goal was simply to make this an attractive room that we could appreciate in the warmer months of the year.

We made this room habitable, but it wasn't what we had in mind for its ultimate use. Two years later we took the renovation of this room to the next level and created what we call "The Tree House".

The picture on the right shows us converting the room to a year-round room with floor-to-ceiling windows. We did most of the work ourselves, saving thousands of dollars. Although we had professionals install the windows and upgrade the electricity, we insulated, hung the sheet rock, taped, and finished the room ourselves.

The picture above shows the view into our kitchen as it was with a large window over the sink and a door to the porch.

The picture below shows it as it is now! We removed the window over the sink and opened up the view considerably. We removed the door so that the Tree House is now part of the kitchen.

Now that the room has been converted, my husband and I agree it is one of the very best modifications we have made. We find we are living in this room everyday. A 19thC pine scrub table is where we have dinner every night. Because the room is at a second-story level, we can watch the birds fly by and look down at the expanse of perennial gardens I have planted. Watching a storm come across the lake or the swans swim by is a real treat. This room gives you the feeling that you are right out on the lake, but without the bugs and heat of summer. You can see why we call this "The Tree House"!

There's more room for display too! The theorem paintings are two pieces of a large collection by the late Ann Rea. Her work is displayed in the American Folk Art Museum and The White House Library. The carved figures are from Germany. The expression on the faces of the German couple on the napkin rings is delicate and extraordinary!

Tip #29

If you see a good bench, buy it! Just as cutting boards have endless possibilities, so do benches, stools, or crickets. A customer asked me the difference between a stool and cricket. To my knowledge, a cricket has an "apron" on the sides, whereas a bench or stool just has a flat piece of board. As you can see, I use crickets or benches for numerous purposes. I enjoy creating different visual planes and heights.

Old buckets are great too!

The chippy white bench below serves
as a coffee table in "The Tree House."
The antique spindle on the table was
used to sew brims on hats.

One advantage to collecting country and
using old painted pieces as furniture is
that it's difficult to "hurt them." I even
tell my guests, with a smile, not to worry
because any marks will only age the piece
further and add value.

Don't be afraid to adapt your furniture to fit your needs! There are a few pieces of furniture that I have purchased with two thoughts in mind; I appreciate their warmth as an antique and I want them to serve a practical purpose. The antique pine cupboard houses a stereo, CD player, and tapes. I have other cupboards that house a TV. Unfortunately, old cupboards were not made to house modern media equipment. They are not deep enough to allow a piece of equipment to fit inside and still be able to close the door. My personal preference is that stereos and televisions are not visible in my rooms. I purchased the cupboard pictured on the left for the practical purpose of holding equipment. I knew that I would not resell the piece and that I was compromising the value and integrity of it when I removed the back and cut out a shelf. I'm pleased with the result and would much rather have a piece of furniture which fits the period style of my home.

Another well-spent $10. The galvanized tub is filled with dried magnolia leaves from a friend's tree. This sits in my entrance hall. I add varied dried berries to it depending on the season – bittersweet in the fall, cockscomb in the winter, and clusters of dried spring flowers in the spring and summer.

The empty clock case was found
in an old barn and purchased for
$10. The paper lining is original, but
obviously the clock is gone. I cleaned
up the original 19thC wavy glass and
painted the case New England Red by
Sturbridge Paints®. It now is used to
display sets of porcelain berry bowls
and saucers that were hand painted
by my great aunt.

Tip #31

Deck the halls! The family room
downstairs was the last room to complete.
Rather than having a family room, we elected
to use it as my office where I could photograph
items for sale and maintain the holiday shop
for my annual Open House Holiday Sale in the
Fall. The Open House starts the holiday season
for Marsh Homestead Country Antiques. It also
necessitates my beginning to trim the house for
the holidays in September.

*We removed the woodstove, replaced the
carpeting with pine plank flooring, painted
the trim Plantation Red Paint by Old
Village Paints® We then converted the
room to a Christmas shop.*

It's an early season at the Condon house! The Holiday Shop is open for one week before moving all the remaining holiday items to the Southern Star Shop in Nellysford. However, the entire house is open and trimmed.

A German feather tree sits on the churn table in the living room. I decorate this 38 inch-high tree with a variety of 1.5-inch vintage German ornaments as well as Putz animals and buildings.

I decorate eight trees each year and each one has its own theme or style. The country tree in the living room is filled with unique country ornaments. There are no glass ornaments, but rather quilted pieces or handmade pieces that I've received as gifts from family and friends over the years. A 19thC rocking horse sits to the side and an old lighted village with a trolley is set up under the tree to the wonder of the grandchildren.

The tree in the dining room is trimmed in the Victorian era. Vintage ornaments, many from Germany and many hand blown, decorate this tree. The angel tree topper is lighted and dates to the 1940's. The wreath over the mantel was made with Shiny Bright® vintage ornaments.

The hand-made stockings by Kathy Lombardi are filled with miniature packages, berries, and other holiday items. Some are just filled with coal! These are one of my most popular items sold at the Open House Holiday Sale.

The partridge sits atop this folky primitive pear tree surrounded by cloth and German Putz animals.

This 3-foot twig tree is trimmed with vintage German ornaments and lighted with vintage bubble lights. Each tree is special. While I enjoy this one for the bubble lights and the memories they evoke, my grandchildren are more fascinated by it than I am!

The view from the front hall into the dining room. The hooked-rug saltbox house on the wall is a favorite, which I cannot claim to have made.

I like the use of fruit in my holiday displays. I also like to create Williamsburg decorations similar to that on the front of the mantel.

The same great-grandfather who had made the dollhouse in the upstairs landing, made this water powered Christmas tree stand out of cigar boxes for my grandmother in 1885 when she was a little girl. The water comes down from the mountain over the water wheel

which operates the stone grinders by moving them up and down. At the same time, the water flows down the stream and the power manipulates the woman's arms so it looks as though she is milking a cow. The water then flows into a pond in the fenced-in farm yard.

When my parents downsized, I was given the dollhouse and my brother received the Christmas tree stand.

The adage "a copy is never as good as the original" certainly proves true in the case of my attempt to duplicate what my great-grandfather had done. My tree stand is made with rough lumber rather than cigar boxes. It was fun to build and it gives me a place to display my Putz animals. The tree is trimmed with small white lights berries and over fifty feathered birds of different colors and varieties.

As the water wheel turns, the stone grinders chop up and down. The farmer is a German carved piece and the stonecutter's house was made out of a birdhouse that I covered with pebbles from the driveway.

The pond was created using a water pump found in nurseries for small indoor fountains. It bubbles and creates a gurgling sound. The water is recycled from a bucket beneath the stand. All of the animals are German Putz animals and have been collected over time. The woman is a German carved figure and is carrying a small basket of eggs.

The "green room" is ready to welcome holiday guests. The feather tree at the foot of the bed sits atop a 19thC blanket chest in red wash.

I use German feather trees in each of my rooms. They vary in size and color, but in each case, they are surrounded by German woolly stick-legged sheep.

The Old World Santa in green velvet is another one of Kathy Lombardi's creations. The Santa made with pinecones is also Kathy's.

19thC children in Germany viewed Belsnickel, a servant of Saint Nicholas, with hesitation. While he would carry cookies or candy in a sack, he also carried a cluster of branches for those children who had been bad. No country holiday season would be complete without a Belsnickel collection!

An authentic Belsnickel collection will be valued in the thousands of dollars. My collection has been accumulated over time and is representative of authentic pieces.

The houses are part of a German collection. The 10-inch feather tree has half-inch vintage ornaments from Germany on its branches.

The two Belsnickels on the far right are actually replica candy containers.

I love decorating with snowmen. In the living room, there are three feather trees. The feather tree on the chest is adorned with very small German vintage ornaments, each measuring only one inch. The garland and lights across the mantel front are left intact throughout the year. A crackling fire and lighted mantel on a cold winter's night makes for a cozy and peaceful room.

Stack anything you can! Not only does a stack of collectibles add dimension to your room, it saves on space. The stack can be used for practical purposes as well.

My stack of pantries has taken years to collect. I prefer boxes with dry paint. I substitute or replace each box as a unique color or size is found.

The hooked rug adds texture to the room and blends beautifully with the colors in the stack. While the background looks black, it is actually a combination of dark blues.

*The stack of bail handle pantry
boxes in original dry blue paint
is one of my favorite collections. It
complements the 19thC Stepback
cupboard in blue found in Maine.
A German Noah's Ark is found
on the top shelf surrounded by
German sheep. The hanging iron
candleholder is a reproduction.
The gourd and dried Tansy add
tones of mustard to the room.*

A stack of benches provides an ideal spot for one of Kathy's primitive Raggedy Ann dolls.

The stack to the right was created to make a side table next to a chair in the living room. An early document box in original red paint is placed atop a tall 19thC red bench. It provides just enough space for a 19thC candle box with lollipop handle, a small light, and a cup of tea.

Tip #33 ***Use textures!*** Textures can be found in many forms! Kathy's dolls and animals certainly add an element of texture in almost every room. Hooked rugs provide delightful colors as well as texture. Vintage quilts are always a favorite of collectors.

Below, a hooked rug by Sue Jones of Georgia in luscious colors of gold and sage!

Even bay leaves and pomegranates are great textures!

One of my favorite textures is my faux fruit. Here, on a 19thC washtub in original red wash, sits my grandmother's yellowware bowl filled with faux apples. When my grandchildren ask if they can have an apple, they look bewildered when I tell them "I'm sorry Grammy doesn't have any apples!"

I'll end where I began! These pictures show how far I've come with my rug hooking!

The hooked rug on the left, patterned after an Ohio coverlet, is a copyrighted pattern designed by Edyth O'Neill. It looks fabulous with the original blue screened pie safe found in Ohio.

This rug was adapted from an early 20thC rug I owned.

My hope is that your imagination and creative juices are already beginning to flow. My husband, one evening, observed me pouring through some of my country books and magazines and innocently asked "What do you do? Just look at the pictures?" As you know, sometimes that's all it takes. Hopefully, my ideas and pictures are ones upon which you can build. Those of us who could "wallow in country" share a bond. We are a "community of collectors" eager to exchange ideas, show off our "finds" with pride, welcome strangers to our homes, and gladly share the story behind each treasure with the least bit of encouragement. I've discovered that I am not alone in my obsession to make the most of a day of antiquing! Sustenance is only considered when the last dash of hope has expired and the knowledge that there is no longer an open shop.

I was asked recently if I was almost done with my home. After a pause, I replied that I would probably **never** be done. I will always upgrade, continue to "borrow" or "adopt" from my shop, and redecorate and redecorate. It is a way of life! It is a state of flux that is part of the enjoyment. It gives us that opportunity to nest over and over again. I doubt, however, that I will ever be able to accumulate enough for another book; at least my husband would hope not.

Thanks for allowing me to share my home with you.